Old English Sheeepdogs

at Work

Sabrina Lakes

Herding Dogs

PAWS & PASTURES

at Work

xist Publishing

Check out all of the books in the Paws and Pastures Series

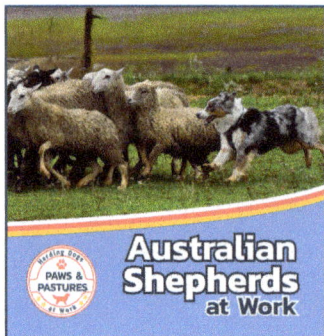

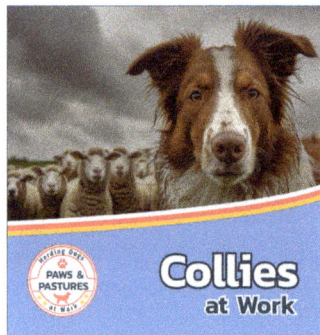

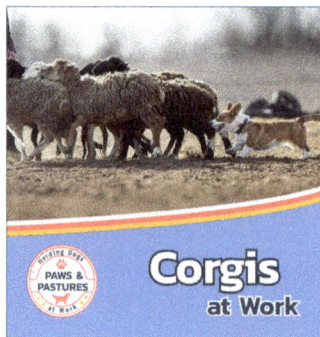

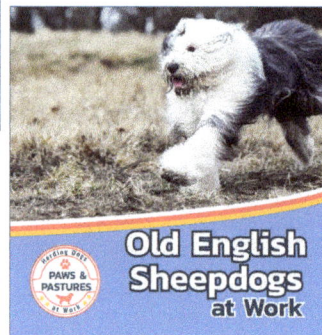

Australian Shepherds at Work

Collies at Work

Corgis at Work

Old English Sheepdogs at Work

Published in the United States by Xist Publishing
www.xistpublishing.com
© 2025 Copyright Xist Publishing

First Edition
Hardcover ISBN: 978-1-5324-5535-3
Paperback ISBN: 978-1-5324-5536-0
eISBN: 978-1-5324-5534-6

PUBLISHED IN TEXAS

Table of Contents

Introduction to Old English Sheepdogs

Old English Sheepdogs are large, fluffy dogs. They have thick fur and a bobtail. They come from England. Farmers used them to help with sheep. Old English Sheepdogs are smart and loving. They enjoy working and spending time with their families.

Fun Facts About Old English Sheepdogs

Old English Sheepdogs are very strong. They can run and play for a long time. Their fur is usually white and gray. Old English Sheepdogs have a lot of energy. Many people love them because they are so gentle and kind.

What is Herding?

Herding means guiding animals like sheep or cows. Old English Sheepdogs help farmers keep animals in groups. They move the animals to new places. This job is very important on farms.

Why Old English Sheepdogs are Great Herders?

Old English Sheepdogs are great herders because they are strong and smart. They learn commands quickly and love to work. Their thick fur keeps them warm in all weather. Old English Sheepdogs are also very brave and can handle big animals. They are always ready to help!

Training an Old English Sheepdog

Training an Old English Sheepdog is fun and rewarding. Start with basic commands like "sit" and "stay." Use treats to reward good behavior. Be patient and kind. Old English Sheepdogs love to learn and enjoy pleasing their owners.

Games to Help Old English Sheepdogs Learn

Games make training enjoyable for Old English Sheepdogs. Play fetch to teach them to come back quickly. Hide treats for them to find using their strong noses. Another fun game is herding a ball, which helps them practice herding skills in a playful way.

A Day in the Life of a Herding Old English Sheepdog

Old English Sheepdogs start their day full of energy. After breakfast, they get ready to work. They help the farmer by guiding the animals out to the fields. Old English Sheepdogs are always eager to start their day.

Working with the Animals

Throughout the day, Old English Sheepdogs work hard. They keep the animals together and make sure they stay safe. They move quickly and use their barks to guide the animals. Old English Sheepdogs are excellent at their job and enjoy every moment of it.

17

Caring for an Old English Sheepdog

Old English Sheepdogs need nutritious food to stay healthy and strong. They eat balanced meals twice a day. Brushing their thick fur regularly keeps it clean and shiny. Trimming their nails helps them run and play without discomfort.

Keeping Your Old English Sheepdog Healthy

Old English Sheepdogs need daily exercise to stay fit. Walks, playtime, and working keep them happy. Regular check-ups at the vet ensure they stay in good health. Old English Sheepdogs love being active and thrive when they have plenty to do.

Old English Sheepdogs at Rest

After a busy day, Old English Sheepdogs need to rest. They enjoy napping in cozy spots to recharge. Resting helps them get ready for another day of work and play. They also like cuddling with their family members.

Fun Activities for Old English Sheepdogs

Even when resting, Old English Sheepdogs love to play. They enjoy toys that squeak or bounce. Puzzle toys challenge their minds and keep them entertained. Spending time with their family is their favorite activity of all.

Glossary

Balanced Meals Nutritious food that keeps dogs healthy and strong.

Commands Words or signals used to tell a dog what to do, like "sit" or "stay."

Exercise Activities like walking or playing that help keep a dog strong and fit.

Grooming Taking care of a dog's fur and nails to keep them clean and healthy.

Herding Guiding and moving animals like sheep or cows.

Nutritious Food that is healthy and good for growth and strength.

Puzzle Toys Toys that challenge a dog's mind and keep them entertained.

Recharge Resting to get energy back after working or playing.

Treats Special food given to dogs as a reward for good behavior.

Index

Keyword List

Nouns	Verbs	Adjectives	Adverbs
animal	are	active	daily
bobtail	come	balanced	easily
command	cuddle	big	quickly
cow	enjoy	brave	regularly
dog	eat	clean	safely
ear	follow	cozy	together
energy	guide	eager	throughout
farmer	have	excellent	
farm	help	fluffy	
field	hide	full	
fun	keep	gentle	
fur	learn	gray	
ground	love	healthy	
job	move	kind	
leg	nap	large	
meal	play	loving	
morning	run	new	
nail	start	patient	
nose	stay	shiny	
people	trim	strong	
sheep	work	thick	

28

Herding Dogs

PAWS &
PASTURES

at Work